Friendship

*The Beautiful Connection to Hold All
Under the Same Umbrella Without Any Restriction*

S Afrose

Ukiyoto Publishing

All global publishing rights are held by

Ukiyoto Publishing

Published in 2023

Content Copyright © S Afrose

ISBN 9789360494346

All rights reserved.
No part of this publication may be reproduced, transmitted, or stored in a retrieval system, in any form by any means, electronic, mechanical, photocopying, recording or otherwise, without the prior permission of the publisher.

The moral rights of the authors have been asserted.

This is a work of fiction. Names, characters, businesses, places, events, locales, and incidents are either the products of the author's imagination or used in a fictitious manner. Any resemblance to actual persons, living or dead, or actual events is purely coincidental.

This book is sold subject to the condition that it shall not by way of trade or otherwise, be lent, resold, hired out or otherwise circulated, without the publisher's prior consent, in any form of binding or cover other than that in which it is published.

www.ukiyoto.com

Dedicated to my Dear Friends-
Specially,

Phyllis Gail, Romeo Della Valle, Alan L Bose, Alan Johnson, Art Abraham, Vasanth Kumar VP, Kumar Prasanna, Drew Clausen, Tess Ritumalta, Gelda Castro, Loi Monroe, Annette Tarpley, Juan Antonio V. Delgadillo, William Warigon, Zlatan Demirovic, Lucille A Laroche, Fatim makki, Lucio Roberto Ramirez Gonzalez, Jose Luis Rubio Zarzuela, Alexander Kabishev, Nadia Toumi.

Thanks a lot dear all for being my friends.
I am so much grateful to all of you. Each word, from your site, helps my write to fly as like as the dreamy kite. How wonderful!

Hope, as like as
You will love me,
You will love my writes,
You will touch my poetic canvas of books.

You will be welcome anytime into this poetic garden of S Afrose. There are 19 poetic flowers of words. Try to see and say any word, as like as the dearest friends.

Take my love as the purest essence of Divine Love.

Acknowledgement

Thanks a lot Dear Almighty for blessing me always.

Thank you so much dear parents, friends, readers, well wishers.

Without yours' supports, I can't make my paradise of the poetic flowers.

I am so so much grateful to this wonderful planet of poetry. After being a part of this planet, I have gotten lots of friends. They are really amazing. We didn't meet each other. We didn't know anyone properly. But the magic of poetry makes a unique connection,
to hold all of us, as dear friends.

"The essence of true friendship is unbeateable"

Hope it will persist forever.

© S Afrose, BD.

Stop and Try to Pick the True Essence of Friendship

The world is lack of love and friendship. It is full of angers, hate, grudges, frustrations, fears. Bloody hawks fly. Tears fallen as the unwanted rainfall. This makes the devastated platform.

Losing the ray of love. Mind can't make any beautiful garden.

Flowers fail to touch any heart. Why and why???

This should be stopped anyway. We must think to stop this nasty part.

The world is losing the sweet essence. Need to resurrect the core of heart.

"Be the friend, each other.

Be the friend for the sweet garden of the world.

Friendship… the mandatory ring to take and

Make the evergreen connection between all the people."

Friendship... a poetry book, reflects the core messages about the friendship, the true essence of the friendship.

For example- Friendship (I), The Beautiful Umbrella, Negative Thoughts etc.

Hope you will be able to get special essences of this poetic flower.

(For any kind of unexpected words, just forgive)

Thanks!

From Author Desk ♥

© S Afrose, BD.

3rd Dec-23

Contents

Almighty Is The Best Friend	1
Friendship (I)	3
What Is Friendship?	5
The Beautiful Umbrella	7
Negative Thoughts	9
Deep In Pain	11
The Flame Of Friendship	13
The Bonfire	15
True Or False?	17
Yellow Rose	19
Burning Burden	21
Calling Dear Friends	23
Let's Celebrate	25
Your Best Friend	27
Rainbow Heart	30
The Long Way	32
Dear Planet	34
Time To End	35
Spring Peeps	36
An Exceptional Friendship	38

My Friend	40
This Is The best Moment	42
Special Day	46
Respect And Love	49
Think Before Doing Anything	51
My Dear Lovely Friend	53
He Or She	55
Share To Be Relaxed	57
Make Sure This Time	59
Have This	61
Dear Mommy, The Best Friend.	62
Honestly Saying	65
The Real Gem	67
Lucky, I Am.	69
Friendship (II)	71
About the Author	73

Almighty Is The Best Friend

Don't forget,
Almighty is your best friend.

Don't forget
To bow down dearself, to Him.

Don't forget
To love and respect with sincere prayer.

When everything turns to be your enemies,
Recall those moments of pleasure.

Friendship

Almighty is everywhere,
To be with you,
To hold your hands,
As the dearest one.

(29th Nov-23)

Friendship (I)

The wonderful platform
With sound of words and senses,
With joyous arts, care, share etc.
That's the fragrance of friendship.

A bond with so many rings,
A bond with so many arts,
A bond with so many wings,
A bond with lots of love.

All must be welcome
As usual,
To be here,
To make the best platform of friendship.

Yes dear all,
It's true.

Friendship

The best platform of life,
The desired panel to hold all under the same umbrella.

(24th Nov-23)

What Is Friendship?

People,
Some chit-chat,
Beautiful time flies,
Messages from the deepest core of minds.

Mind says loudly-
Not fair.
No, it's not fair.

Then come on,
And pay your kind attention,
Hold this hand,
Friendship, the desired lane.

Fragrance of mind
Can get,
From the core of zephyr.

Friendship

Everything turns out, for what?

You know that,
You know dear,
It's the friendship,
Take this vow at last.

Never forget
What do you see?
What do you want?
Lane of friends, my dear.

(25th Nov-23)

The Beautiful Umbrella

It's the beautiful umbrella.
To hold all,
To protect all,
From the unwanted rainfall.

It's the beautiful umbrella.
When someone will come
To be here,
Can get the desired kite.

It's the beautiful umbrella.
Come on dear,
See and verify,
What do you want?

It's not only for you,
It's not only for me,

Friendship

It's all over,
It's for all of us.

Yes dear!
It's the umbrella of friendship.
It's the umbrella of friendship.
Forget any rift.
It's the umbrella of friendship!

When you will see this,
You will get the chance,
Holding always,
It's the magical stick.

It's the beginning of the happiness.
It's the beginning of the mind.
It's the umbrella of friendship.
It's the precious part of dear earth.

(28th Nov-23)

Negative Thoughts

Negative thoughts!
Holding you
Always,
You can't stand up.

Ah!
So sad.
So painful.
This is not right to hold on.

Need to clear,
Your thoughts, your layer.
Now it's time,
To stand up,
Holding hands of friendship,
Yes, my dear!

Friendship

He or she
As your Friends,
Now coming,
To wipe your tears.
Negative thoughts, oops!
Go to hell, nasty shells.

Friend, I am.
Pls relax.
Share your pain,
Share your thoughts,
I am here as your friend,
To erase all the pains,
To wipe your tears.

(24th Nov-23)

Deep In Pain

When pain comes
As a snake,
To grasp
The desired heart;
Call your friend
To be here,
To hear your crying heart.
Your favourite mind, lays down.
This time is so harmful to move on,
All alone.

Mind fails
To take
Any decision,
As the fruitful way.
Sharing and caring
With the dear friends,

Friendship

So vital.
To show the way,
For the better part,
At last.

The snake can't be able to bite you dear.
If can,
Then you may have the chance,
To make this time,
To support port of life.
For saving dear self
From the fallen strike,
With the power of friendship,
Holding the hands of dear friend.

Just feel this time as usual,
You will realize.

(25th Nov-23)

The Flame Of Friendship

Stare!
Why?

It's the flame of friendship!
It's the flame of friendship!

Stars, we are.
We know, you know.

It's the very special thing.
Hi dear!

See and feel,
How can gain this time?

Friendship

Stars, all the day,
Stars we are.

(25th Nov-23)

The Bonfire

The bonfire
Here,
You enjoy
With your friends.

Make sure
It's safe,
For all;
No harmful arts.

Of course,
The bonfire of the friends.

Don't be the crazy ones,
Don't be cruel,
To destroy any part,
Which is a maze of your life.

Friendship

The bonfire of the friendship!
The bonfire of your dream!

(25th Nov-23)

True Or False?

Make sure
This time,
Which one is True or False?

True friends
Or False friends?

There are many more
To act,
As like as the friends.
Faked!

They wear masks.
You fail to see the real faces.
Can't discover,
Can't believe, at last.

Friendship

It's your time
To make the mind.

Which one is true
Which one is false?

Answer?

Ask yourself?
In front of the eyes, what can you see?

Will get the answer,
If you take your time
To think thoroughly,
To differentiate these terms-

True or False?

(25th Nov-23)

Yellow Rose

Enjoying,
Hurray!

Hopping,
Jolly ray!

This is the day of life.
Yellow roses all over.

Let this time stop,
Show the world.

Yellow rose!
The fragrance of heart.
It helps to show
The joyous world,

With dear friends,
All the time.

(25th Nov-23)

Burning Burden

So many tasks,
So tough.
Shift the mind,
For some moments.
And then
It will be fine.

Hurray!
Hope,
Hip-hop.

Burning the burden,
Burning part,
Burning life.

Wow!
How?

Friendship

My friends,
Come on and help,
To take the decision,
Of the desired part.

So, so tough?
So, what?
Now can feel,
The Joyous life.

(25th Nov-23)

Calling Dear Friends

Friends for life,
Essence of life.

Friends for life,
Essence of the time.

Calling dear friends,
Seeing the lane.

The staircase is on going
And mind can't get the courage to move on.

Oh dear Almighty!
Pls help.

Friendship

Hey!
Will you be my friend?
Friend?

How?
It's good to hear,
Or bad,
Don't know?

But I am lonely
I need a true friend,
True friendship,
For the smooth Journey of life.

(29th Nov-23)

Let's Celebrate

Today is another one,
Special column, special balm.
What's that?

Happy Friendship Day!

Let's celebrate,
This day.

Knit,
Knot of thoughts.

Friends,
A dreamy pool!

Frustrated arts?
Just give up.

Friendship

Hi!
This is the plot of your mind.

Friend!
Be the friend of your mind.
Be the friend of yourself.
Your well-wisher,
A sweet crane.

(26th Nov-23)

Your Best Friend

Friend?
Not so silly
To say.
To hold this part
To be the best one.

Yes!
The best friend!
Your best friend!

Who will share and care,
Respect as dear,
Without any fear,
Without any tease.

Anyone from any site,
If there's someone,
Can think,
You are the luckiest person,
My dear!

As
It's rare,
To get someone,
As the best friend,
Till the death.

Wow!
How sweet!
A little blink,
Friend or best friend?
What do you want to say?

Mostly
To mind,
Your well-wisher,
As close as the deepest heart,
As the crucial part of your life.

There,
You can be relaxed,
You can get soberness,
You feel so chill,
To forger any disastrous panel.

(28th Nov-23)

Rainbow Heart

Ready?
This time,
You will see dear earth.

Rainbow heart!
Rainbow heart!

Ready?
This time,
You will get that touch.
Rainbow love!

Rainbow heart!
Midst the world,
Muse of words.

Muse of colours,
All are here.
Rainbow, dear!

(24th Nov-23)

The Long Way

So far

A ray,

The long way.

So far

You say,

The long bay.

So far

We want,

Holding this ray.

So far

The way,

The long bay.

Once
It was here,
The bay of ray.

Now have to realize,
People don't destroy this clay.

Come on and play,
Lay and lay,

As the flying dreams,
The Butterflies' Bay.

(24th Nov-23)

Dear Planet

To make
To hold,
To be the bold one.
No rush
No dust,
No grasping moment, at all.

Dear platform!
Dear planet!
Don't make this choice.

I know.
You know,
What is the Happiness?

(24th Nov-23)

Time To End

Don't forget
It's time
To end,
This part
The windy touch,
Winter's love.

Time to end!
Time to welcome someone else.
Who knows?
Who is the scapegoat?
Who is the best?

(24th Nov-23)

Spring Peeps

Time to come
To sing
To dance,
To welcome-

Spring peeps.
Spring loves.

Hello dear!
Hello dear!

I am here.
Come on and see,
A new bee.

It's your peer.
Peeps,
As the basking art.

This is true.
You know, how is that?
As your dreamy friend,
It's the Spring's Love.

(24th Nov-23)

An Exceptional Friendship

Two friends
They are not familiar.

They meet.
Some chit-chat.
And then…

Two friends,
Wow!
They are best friends.

They can't depart.
Destiny smirks.
Universe gives the best award
As the soulmates, forever.

Both of them,
Enjoy the trend of this lane.

The Paper and the Pen!
They are the best friends
An exceptional friendship.

A pen and a white paper!
They play.
They sing,
They dance.
They share their feelings.
They care,
They love.
They hold each other
Tightly,
Mutual understanding, how nice!

(29th Nov-23)

My Friend

Little butterfly!
What's your mission?
Can tell me.

Little one!
You are so adorable,
Make me your dear friend.

My dear lovely friend.
I'm very simple,
You see that.

Little one!
I love the simplicity,
Like the moon in the sky.

We can make a history
Friendship, such a gossamer,
Embracing heartfelt touches, forever..

(29th Nov-23)

This Is The best Moment

Morning!
A call-
Hello, dear hearts!
Where are all of you?
Don't hide, just come and see,
This Miracle.

Darkness is no more.
Sun smiles.
Golden shades of sweet life.
They are playing within your hearts.

Two friends!
Evergreen parts.
What a lovely quote!
We're two friends.

Lots of hopes,
Flowing dreams.
Blooming life,
Ray of positivity.
Though, there are so many strifes,
Still the strength of friendship… unbelievable.

Two friends!
This is the best moment of life.

(25th Nov-23)

Canvas

Artist?
No.
But, want to draw?
Yes!

The brush and the canvas.
Reflection of the mind.

Painting with Lost Sense,
The canvas is the mirror of mind.

It reflects,
All the hidden sights.

The brush moves.
How can cope the absent mind?

The blurred vision,
Hidden emotions.

A story of flash fiction.
Addiction or affection,
Whatever?
Superficial!

A profound sense.

A picture!
Oh no!
What's that?

My lost paradise!
Still persists,
Deepest, the mind.

(29th Nov-23)

Special Day

That day is very special.
Soaked in deep pain.

No dear one, near.
All alone,
Midst the darkness.

Quivering heart!
Unwanted fear!
Unfathomable situation!

Life, in dredly shell.
Kneel down.
A silent urge!
For what?

A voice is heard,
Someone calling.
Who are you?
Why do you cry?
Open the eyes and look at me-
"I'm your friend"

Raise your head.
Hold my hands.
Don't worry,
Trust me.
I can help you.
You have to believe this.

A tiny hope touches my heart.
Oh dear Almighty!
Are you there?
Or an angel to help?
Or a ghost, wants to grasp my soul?

Hahahaha!
How silly thoughts!
I'm a mere human like you.
Stucked here, a long period.
Now the sun peeps,
We can find out the way to move on.

That moment, I get my spirit again.
Stand up.
Its presence, a great turn.

A little chit-chat!
A new bond between two souls
Like the friendship, the promise.
To hold each other for the safe turn.

(25th Nov-23)

Respect And Love

No single space exists,
No single word can evoke.

When heart sings the song of life,
By showering petals of friendship and love,
Don't need to argue with anyone,
You will get the precious treasure.

Respect and love!

Some silly fissures,
Some hidden darts.
Trying to spoil the value of heart.
Never lose the temple of integrity.

Wait, with patience and love.
Finally the crescent verse of true friendship!

Respect and love!

(29th Nov-23)

Think Before Doing Anything

The position of your life,
Not totally fine,
All the time.

You have to think,
Before doing anything,
Just think twice.

Your friend is here,
Your favourite mind,
Tour of life.

Don't forget
Everything is here,
To be your peers.

Friendship

You have to think
Again and again,
It's your time.

(3rd Dec-23)

My Dear Lovely Friend

Broken mind!
Midnight vibe,
Hello!

Broken mind!
Midnight calls,
Oh no!

Broken mind!
At least,
Say hi.

My dear lovely friend.
Who is that one?
My dear!

Your favourite song!
Your favourite tune!
Your favourite book, my dear.

(3rd Dec-23)

He Or She

Nothing can beat
This time,
When it's essential to wear
Crown of mind.

He or she
Not a matter,
Holding hands
Of dear mind.

He will be your friend
He will be your smile.

She will be your friend
She will be your smile.

Friendship

Friendship is such an art,
Anything turns into the rainbow hub.
Anyone can be the painter,
Anything can turn into sweet art.

Not a matter,
No gender bias,
Be loyal, be respectful,
Be the friend, each other.

Be the friend.
Be the true friend.
Be the ward of trust,
He or she, doesn't matter.

(3rd Dec-23)

Share To Be Relaxed

Deep in pain
That makes you,
A living hell.

You can't live
As like as.

You have to share
With someone,
To be relaxed.

Share with your
Dear friend.
It will help
To relax your mind.

That's the magic of friendship.
That's the magic of real friend.

It helps anyone
To share anything,
To seek serenity, at least.

(3rd Dec-23)

Make Sure This Time

Probably not fair,
If you escape
This time.

Make sure this time,
You will be the friend
Of your child.

Your child,
Is your pride;
You have to say this word.

He or she
Needs a hand of friend,
As you are parent,
You have been there always.

A parent is the best friend
Of the children,
Little or elder,
For all... the same trend.

(3rd Dec-23)

Have This

Wear this ring.
Have this.
You love it,
Your favourite seat.

Consider,
When time seeks
The helpline,
For your smile.

Your friend!
Your favourite song.
Needs your attire,
You have to give this time.

(3rd Dec-23)

Dear Mommy, The Best Friend.

Today I will not cry,
Today I will say the world,
My dear lovely friend,
My dear parents.
My dear mother!

Fear, to be there?
Mom comes, near.
Saying some words,
You're brave, my dear.

Dear Mommy, the best friend.
Dear Mommy, the best friend.

Sick, I am.
Can't make my reading time.

This time,
The exam is ahead.

My friend my mom,
Comes
And says,
Help your mind.

Your health is the prime concern.
Exam... oh no, dear!
I know you will,
As you don't scare anymore.

That's the mental support,
From each friend,
Your true friend.
Your best friend.

Dear Mommy, the best friend!

(3rd Dec-23)

Honestly Saying

To be the winner-
Literally, for a paper?

Not right?
Be good,
Be honest.

What do you need?
What do you learn,
From this part?

The core message-
Be the friend,
Of your dreamy world.

Then you can be the winner,
Itself.
With all sweet essences,
You know that.

(3rd Dec-23)

The Real Gem

When true friend
Comes to your mind,
You will find out
The real gem,
Who is here or there?

A true friend!
Makes the sense
To forget any pain,
To heal the hidden scar
Of your mind.

The real gem!
Yes, it's the real gem.
When you will think,
You can realise,
It's obviously right.

(3rd Dec-23)

Lucky, I Am.

I will say this always.
How lucky I am!
To be here
To get you,
As my dear friend.

Of course I agree,
I am so lucky.
Your each word
Touches my mind,
I can get up.

Life!
In deep pain
Or success,
You always gear up,
My wheels of mind.

Lucky, I am.
To get you
As my friend.
Yes!
I will say this always.

You're my best friend.
You're my true friend.
You are my panacea.
Lucky I am, to hold your hands.
My dear lovely friend... Poetry Realm!

(3rd Dec-23)

Friendship (II)

Friends' Ship
Friendship!

Real Time
Reality of World.

Inter-transaction
Intra-transaction.

Entire the World
Enter, my dear.

Need to Reflect
Need to Revive the Lost World.

Den of your Mind.
Deep Sleep, not approved this time.

Friendship

Ship, the Mystic Ship.
Ship of your Dreams.

Hello! Wake up.
Hello! Come on.

Instantly you see,
It's your World.

Past to Present,
Prepare Yourself.

Friendship.
Friends for the Bluish Lovely Universe.

(3rd Dec-23)

About the author

S Afrose

Author S Afrose (Sabiha Afrose, from Bangladesh) has made her writing realm since August-2020.

She has been enjoying, each of the parts, of this writing ward. She tries to express the hidden word or emotion, by her words; with the glamour of poetry. Poetry is her best friend. Her writes have been publishing on magazines and anthologies (80+). In this writing realm, she has achieved many awards (beyond her expectations eg. Doctorate in Literature from Instituto Cultural Colombiano, Literoma Laureate Winner 2022, Mahatma Gandhi Award 2023 from Instituto Cultural Colombiano, One of the World Record Holders for Hyperpoem, etc.)

Published author of poetry books- **Thanks Dear God, Poetic Essence , Reflection of Mind , Glittering Hopes, Angels Smile, Tiny Garden of Words, Dancing Alphabet, Artistic Muse,**

Essence of love, The Magical Quill, Dear Children, Haunted Site. Woman, The Butterfly, A Little Fantasy, Lion's Roar, The Bride, No War, Lost Lotus.

All are available worldwide (on Amazon.com & from publication hub and from other sites-Flipkart, Bookshop, Booksgoogle, Barnesandnobles etc. also, as any format). Apart these, there are some Bengali and English poetry books (available on rokomari.com in Bangladesh).

Her mother is Selina Begum and father is Manirul Islam.
Educational achievements- B Pharm, M Pharm from Jahangirnagar University, Bangladesh.
Hobbies are reading, writing, specially the paradise of the poetic flowers.

Contact- afrosewritings@outlook.com, sabiha_pharma@yahoo.com
You Tube: S Afrose *Muse of Writes*(@safrose_poetic_arts)
Facebook page: Muse of Words by S Afrose
Twitter:@afrose2020
Inst. @safrosepoetryworld

"THANK YOU SO MUCH"

FROM AUTHOR DESK

BANGLADESH

www.ingramcontent.com/pod-product-compliance
Lightning Source LLC
LaVergne TN
LVHW041539070526
838199LV00046B/1746